I0212463

I'm Saved.
So, Now What?

SHAY HARRIS

RIVERHOUSE PUBLISHING, LLC
MEMPHIS

I'm Saved. So, Now What?

RiverHouse Publishing, LLC
1509 Madison Avenue
Memphis, TN 38104

Copyright © 2019 by Shay Harris

All rights reserved. No part of this book may be reproduced, stored in a retrieval system or transmitted in any form or by any means without written permission of the Publisher, excepting brief quotes used in reviews.

All **RiverHouse Publishing, LLC** Titles, Imprints and Distributed Lines are available at special quantity discounts for bulk purchases for sales promotions, premiums, fund-raising and educational or institutional use.

First RiverHouse, LLC Trade Paperback Printing: 1/24/2019

ISBN: 978-1-7335622-0-1

www.RiverHousePublishingLLC.com

This book is dedicated to the three women who've influenced my life the most & my father:

My mother, Shirley Harris, whose love, wisdom, no-nonsense discipline, genuine care, and belief in me have been the wind beneath my wings. Mom, you've so become my best friend as I've matured. You're tested, I've tried you, and you've been the truth. Thank you for believing in me when no one did. Thank you for wiping my forehead when I was sick. Thank you for teaching me your style. I swear I think if I hadn't come along, you'd be a fashion model, writer, and so much more yourself. But instead you poured yourself into me. You gave me a chance. Thank you from the bottom of my heart!

Both Grandmothers, Mary Harris & Mosetta Bew, whose love and hugs I miss dearly. Their love of family gave me a love for family. Their service to church and community is indwelled within me through those days of helping to clean our church, helping cook on Saturdays for church Sunday church fellowships.

Speaking of cooking I am so grateful to my MaDear Mosetta for passing her love of cooking on to me. It was her love language, one that I am honing and have learned to also speak that language. The ingenuity of Grandma Mary to just create things has also been a saving grace for me. I can find a way to fix anything thanks to her. My creative bones, my seriousness for caring for people, my belief in myself, I thank my mother for. She laid down her own dreams of being a writer to become and wife and mother to cover me.

I'm forever grateful. My walk with God was a non-negotiable. These women made sure I learned early who God was, therefore, rooting and grounding me early. All that I am came from somewhere great. The world doesn't know how great they are so I must tell the world. These three praying, God-fearing, soul-food queens, with the ability to get anything done have been my rocks. The lessons I've learned the character I've gained-I attribute to you all. You remain my backbones…knitted and glued. I thank you.

Anyone who knows me knows I couldn't end this dedication without my Father & Daddy, James E. Harris. Next to God he's been the most important man in my life. He is my heart. My protector. My friend. My fishing instructor. My first boyfriend. He taught me how to small jobs...like who knew I could fix a toilet. LoL! Who knew I could use a hammer & a nail? Daddy, taught me. He didn't take away my love for baby dolls, fairy tales, & the prince who'd rescue me he just made sure I knew there was more than that. He made sure I knew there was more in me. He taught me that a man's actions towards me reveal the man's heart towards. He's not perfect, no man is; but he's my solid. Unchanging. Yes, you have a few lines in your face that say you've changed can & you may not be as muscular as you once were, but Daddy I've never seen you stronger or more loving. It's a blessing to still have a father who rises early every morning & studies his Bible & covers his family

Thank you, Daddy! You've been a wonderful Father & I love you to life!

With all my heart!!!

Acknowledgments

I humbly acknowledge that this book was a divinely inspired work. I was given the mandate to write the book during a time of wrongful job loss, eviction, loss of people that I loved, and thought would always be there, a legal battle, an attack on my health and a few other negatives that the enemy was using to discourage me from focusing on the writing this book. I submit that it was Him, and Him alone who downloaded every word I wrote into my spirit in the wee hours of many mornings.

I'm also very grateful to my ministry mentors for covering me and seeing gifts within me that you were determined, in some way, to help me birth.

Apostle DeWayne Hunt of Abundant Grace Fellowship Church thank you for welcoming me into your music ministry, theatrical ministry, and as a young leader in one of Memphis' most respected church communities. You & First Lady Diane are some of the most creative ministry leaders I've known. God is using you to continue doing new things.

My Spiritual Mom, Apostle Jocyln Franklin of Spiritual Force Ministries, is a fire starter. You are a blessing to me on so many levels. Thank you for challenging me to accept my ministry mantel. Thank you for always covering me in prayer and for speaking life into me. You are amazing!

Pastor Marvin Jackson of the River of Life Church, thank you, for seeing God's anointing on my life. You & First Lady Deborah welcomed me into your music ministry as well as the media ministry. I appreciate you for allowing me to be used in service at The River. Thank you for teaching me about the Bible in ways that blew my mind. Thank you for making me think.

Thank you all for being great teachers and ministry leaders. Thank you for pouring into me during seasons in which God placed you over me to cover me as one of your sheep. Your teachings have inspired me to continue getting to know God more deeply and to do what He called me to do.

He's so dope & so are you!

Table of Contents

PREFACE

I was saved a long time before I knew what being saved really meant. Some well-intended preachers, with erroneous teaching, left me carrying a mountain of guilt, shame, and feelings of unworthiness. They didn't know they were spreading fear through their fire and brimstone, performance-based messages. Growing up, I remember the older generation singing songs about how when they "got saved" & met the Lord they changed. This wasn't just an inside change, but "their hands looked new and their feet did too" according to the songs they'd sing. So, I had this vision in my head of what salvation must really look like. When I got saved none of these outward changes happened to me. I can recall even looking at my hands that day expecting to "see" change. I was twelve years old, and I'll never forget skipping hand-in-hand all the way to my Grandmother Mosetta Bew's home with my cousin, Tammi. We were so happy and excited about this new salvation that we were now a part of.

I went through the scriptural process of salvation and I knew something had happened inside of me, but I didn't really know what to do with what

I had acquired. I was converted and clueless really. Churches are doing a much better job of guiding new Christians through the conversion process of going from a "sinner to a saint", but some still make it so much harder than I believe God ever intended for it to be.

After being a Christian for years and observing what happens once sinners are converted, I believe more effort should come from seasoned Christians and the church to help newly converted Christians along the journey. There are some basic essential behaviors that believers have to plug into in order to navigate through living the Christian life to keep from falling back into old habits and going astray; thus, allowing the enemy to get a foothold on them. Some of these things took many years for me to learn, because I had to unlearn a lot of what I'd learned previously growing up. One thing is certain, had I known them I could've saved myself a lot of years of condemnation, guilt, and hopelessness.

My hope is that this book helps you save the valuable time, stress, and heartbreak that many of us lost and suffered through trying to meet un-required standards and rules that have nothing to do with being a son or daughter of The Living God. This is not the end-all be-all book on Christianity in any way. The Holy Bible is the only authority on your Christian new birth and life as a

Christian. This book is a simple guide past and through the things your flesh and your mortal enemy will throw at you in attempts to make you question your salvation. This information is based on the shortfalls and mistakes I made along the way and the mistakes of other people I've encountered. The hope is that you spend less years looking at your faults and shortcomings, and more years putting the power of the word to work in your everyday life while looking at God and what His Son Jesus did dying on the cross for you more than 2,000 years ago.

CHAPTER 1

T*he greatest gift to you is proof of God's love for you.* As a journalist I've met thousands of people over the years. I've told many people's stories, some of tragedies and triumphs. One thing I realized is that the presence or absence of God in a person's life makes a difference. I basically spent most of my years covering major crimes and politics. I also told feature stories which are usually the feel-good stories where people have gone through something that challenged their core being, like sickness, accidents, and extenuating circumstances that required them to believe in something greater than themselves to overcome.

Being a journalist sometimes requires us to be on the front line right along with police, fire fighters, and other emergency services management teams. In fact, journalists sometimes make it to the scene of the crime or accident before they do. As I said previously, I spent years in the field telling stories. Most of those years were spent covering homicides because I was in urban communities like Memphis & Cleveland, Ohio for years where violence was like a plague. During those times I learned to make the process of covering those stories into ministry. Initially they were hard to cover because of the emotional drain so I found myself asking God to help me to compartmentalize my work and still have compassion, but to not take my work home with me in my mental and emotional chambers. I asked Him to help me handle what I could and to bless people I came in contact with in the field while working. I also asked Him to help me discern where I could and could not help. During those years of getting called out to shootings, murder scenes, and investigative stories that usually left a trail of victims, including their grieving loved ones; I discovered one thing. Most of the victims of the stories I was charged with telling, the people on the scene, and those I interviewed had no idea just how much God loved them. We would get to the scene and sometimes depending on who the victim was, we'd see hundreds of young people and family members standing around trying to grasp their grief as their loved one lay sprawled out on the ground lifeless. As a reporter my job was to get one of these grieving souls to talk to me, hopefully giving my station the one up on the others. This goal quickly grew old for me because it wasn't from God, it was from man. It just didn't feel right. It made the job cold and didn't bless me or my station. So, I knew I needed to bring God in deeper. I made the decision to invite Him into my work situation. I asked Him to help me to be a blessing to His people for as long as He chose to use me in that capacity. I had no idea what I was asking for. There were times I would be the only reporter to get the family members, like that grieving mother whose heart was shattered because her son was supposed to graduate and go to play college ball in a few months. It was like God would bring them to me on the scene or someone in their family would walk up to me and take me to these mothers and they would not only talk to me but embrace me. There were many scenes where we'd embrace, and I would hold them and pray. I sat inside many homes seeing the poverty and pain. In those days listening to the stories of surviving family members and friends I discovered that most of the victims didn't know they were truly loved. Many of them lacked any real hope. It goes without saying that the ones causing this hurt didn't know it either.

I began to realize that if people only knew Him, how much He loves them, and His promises for them that we could turn some of these situations around. At the root of every issue is guilt and condemnation, and a person who's battling with a lack of self-love. Depending on where a person is inside, they'll lose every time because they haven't accepted that the greatest love is the love God gave when He gave His Son to die for every one of us. If you're saved and you don't know that as a Christian you are a part of a royal priesthood (family), you'll look at your current environment or surroundings and think things will never change. If all you see around you makes you feel hopeless, you can't believe.

Poverty, a hard past, or harsh upbringing, sickness and the pain that comes with it, and struggle can cause one to feel that their current situation is all there is. Like where they are is where they're supposed to be; forever living in lack, depression, and always struggling to get ahead. Ultimately this is not true. God's desire is *"that we would prosper and be in good health even as our souls prosper"* according to the word in 3 John 1:2. It doesn't matter who you are or where you've come from, God has a plan for you. Jeremiah 29:11 says it is a good plan to prosper you and not bring you harm, a plan to give you hope and a future. Understanding that every promise of God is for you, no matter your circumstances, is imperative.

Now if you're reading this you've probably already decided to follow Jesus. You've likely already read Romans 10:9 and confessed your sins and believe that Jesus is your Lord and Savior; and that He died for your sins. You probably already believe that God raised Jesus from the dead for you. If this is the case, yeah for you! I am praising

God for you and with you my brothers and sisters in Christ! You've already taken the biggest and most important steps of your lifetime. You are a child of God's! You now have all the rights and privileges other believers have through Christ.

On the flip side, if you haven't made this confession, you can do it now. Set the record straight and make sure you are sure. It's a very simple process and it is the most important step you'll take towards that life God has planned for you. It's not rocket science. God loves us too much to make salvation hard for us.

In the Bible *Matthew 7:9-11* asks, *"Which of you, if your son asks for bread, will give him a stone? Or if he asks for a fish, will give him a snake? If you, then, though you are evil, know how to give good gifts to your children, how much more will your Father in Heaven give good gifts to those who ask Him!"*

God loves you. Let me say it again. God loves YOU! No matter what you've done, no matter where you've come from, no matter how many times you've failed; He loves you. He made salvation easy to gain because He wanted you to have it. In fact, He loves us so much that He sent His Son Jesus to do the hard part of taking on the punishment that stood against our salvation. He loves you so much that He made it a covenant between you and Him. It's not a covenant that anyone else can make for you, and they can't take it from you. He went so far as to say that whosoever calls on the name of the Lord shall be saved. If you ever get a no from God, it is for your own good. The Bible says in *Psalm 84:11* *"No good thing will God withhold from those whose walk is upright"*.

So, a no from Him means what you're asking for is either not in His will which means it's not good for you, or the timing is not right at that moment. He knows that things outside of His will can make life harder for His children. He also knows that in the wrong season of time the right things can be a distraction to His plan for our lives.

The gift of His Son Jesus dying on the cross is the greatest gift He gave to us leading us to salvation. So, you can accept the gift today and get on with living the life He created you to live.

If you are ready to accept this great gift of salvation, don't wait. You can repeat the following prayer and speak the word of God in *Romans 10:9* out loud and immediately become a member of the body of Christ:

Heavenly Father, I am a sinner, but, I believe in my heart that Jesus Christ is Your Son & that You sent Him to die on the cross for me, covering all my sin forever. I believe You raised Jesus Christ from the dead and that He is alive today! So I now repent from my sins and choose to follow and obey Jesus Christ as my Lord and Savior with all my heart for the rest of my life! I thank you, Father that I am now saved by faith in Jesus Christ!

If you just prayed this prayer, "Welcome to the family!" You belong to God and you are a joint heir with Jesus Christ. That means the same things that Jesus did, you can do. The same promises God made in His word are for you; the most important promise being eternal life. So, when you die and we all will one day; you will go to Heaven where you will live forever with the same Jesus Christ Who laid down His life for you. Hell will not be your eternal appointment. You are saved.

Knowing that God loves you changes everything. It changes how you think. It changes how you act. A person who knows who they are in Christ is unlikely to steal from a neighbor or kill someone because they've tapped into knowing there are promises awaiting them that cause them to want nothing to do with lifestyles that lead to hurting other people. The commandment to love our neighbors as we love ourselves is hinged upon this truth. We have to learn to love ourselves, otherwise, we cannot effectively love others. This too is part of the journey of a Christian. None of us came here knowing how to love ourselves. It's a part of the process of knowing God and who we are in Him.

CHAPTER 2

Something wonderful happens when you accept Jesus as Lord of your life. He literally comes to live inside of you once you receive what Jesus did on the cross. Like a computer God downloads His spirit and life into our spirit when we accept Jesus as our Lord and Savior. In the very moment of salvation, we receive the essence of Who He is inside of ourselves. It is His knowing, His mind inside of us. His awesome power begins to permeate every fiber of our being. Each of us becomes a home and vessel that houses God's Spirit when we receive Christ.

In fact, *1 Corinthians 3:16 says "Don't you realize that all of you together are the temple of God and that the Spirit of God lives in you? So you're not only saved when you accept Jesus Christ as your Lord and Savior, He comes to live inside of you."*

He will begin to speak to you in many ways. He speaks to us through His Spirit that dwells in us. He speaks to us as we read the Bible. He speaks to us to give to others. He guides us through urges we have inside to go a different way from His plans for us. His Spirit speaks to us through other people. He speaks to us in dreams and sometimes in the things we see. Even a smell can be God speaking to us. It is, however, up to us to listen.

He does this because He loves us. His ultimate plan for us is relationship with Him. He wants us to grow in the knowledge of Who He Is. He wants us to know Him intimately and to take advantage of all the promises He set before us in His word. Ephesians 3:16-21 is one of my favorite scriptures. Paul was praying for the children of God that "He would grant you, according to the riches of His glory, to be strengthened with might through His Spirit in the inner man, that Christ may dwell in your hearts through faith; that you, being rooted and grounded in love, may be able to comprehend with all the saints what is the width and length and depth and height-to know the love of Christ which passes knowledge; that you may be filled with all the fullness of God."

He wants us to know Him. He knows every single one of us. He knows our thoughts. He knows our desires. He knows the number of hairs on our heads. He knows our struggles. He sees those things we do in secret when no one is watching. He knows our attitudes can sometimes contradict what we say we believe. He knows all the good and bad things about us. Nothing about us is a secret or a surprise to Him. Even still He has a plan for our lives.

That is why when He speaks, it is to our advantage to listen and obey whatever He tells us. Following His plan is the difference between success and failure, operating in power versus everything being a struggle. On our own we carry very limited power, so we struggle to get through life. In Him we have all the power leading us to the life and freedom God has planned.

It doesn't mean there won't be hard days. It means you won't have to go through the hard days by yourself. You have the power of God the Father, Jesus the Son, and God's Holy Spirit working on your behalf. You can literally put the word of God to work in every area of your life.

CHAPTER 3

There is a reason for everything God allows. Many of you had praying mothers, grandmothers, and others who have prayed for you since the day you were born. That is wonderful because so many people have no one. But the fact of the matter is this is personal. It is a personal one on one walk with God; a journey to intimacy.

Yes, God does answer the prayers of the righteous people who are praying for you. However, there comes a time when, by God's design, your journey boils down to you and Him because He wants all of you. So, He can give His all to you. Relationship with Him will never be by force. It has to be your choice once you believe. Don't put your salvation on the shelf. Engage in your relationship with God. Just as you pour into your relationships with people around you, so must you pour yourself into your relationship with God. That's the only way to deepen your relationship.

I'll never forget being off at college without my mother and father to make the hard decisions for me. They couldn't help me make some of my choices. In fact, I remember my mother getting to a point where she stopped making my decisions for me. I'd go to her with a problem or idea expecting her to make up my mind for me and she'd say, "I can't make that decision for you."

She'd tell me, "You know the right thing to do. You know right from wrong." Some of the decisions I faced were strategically allowed by God.

He had started working on me on another level, strengthening me and preparing me for my life walk. Some of what I went through my parents could not help me with. I had to call on the name of the Lord in a way that I'd never had to before.

I had to seek Him for answers and how to navigate through some of the challenges and temptations I faced. While I was in the middle of it, I kept asking God why I was going through it. After it was over, I saw His hand all over it, allowing what the enemy meant to use to break me to be used for my development.

You see, I didn't realize that just as God was there watching over me; the enemy was also watching and plotting out ways to distract me and rip me away from my God given destiny. He'd been watching me since I was a little girl. Even from a very young age he tried to thwart God's plans for me by attacking my emotions and faith in God.

I was a very loving and sweet child, very naïve, and he wanted to destroy the promise on my life.

So, he attacked my body with sickness through tumors and caused me a lot of pain and some deformity during that long season of my life. For 14 years I battled them. I was in and out of hospitals and was told this was something I'd have to live with.

God, in His grace and mercy, was right there. There were moments I asked God to let me die because I couldn't bear the pain, but He wouldn't allow me to give up. Today I can say I am thankful that He wouldn't let me let go. Instead His plan was to heal me, so I could share with others how good He is and that He Is our healer. I had no real concept of healing other than the Bible. God made it real in me by healing me.

God, in no way, caused me to have those tumors. He would never bring sickness on His children. Again, His plans are for our good; to bring us hope and give us a future. The enemy authors every negative storm we face. God speaks peace to the storms and shuts down the winds and waves behind them that try to drown us. His words will guide us out of the raging sea if we allow them to.

You may not have had health issues. But as sure as you're living you will deal with people storms. Like many of you, I've dealt with friends who turned out to be frenemies, been used and deceived, disliked, bullied, and all of those things we experience as human beings in relationship with other human beings. Yet, God was always been right there in it with me, never forsaking me or leaving me. *"Deuteronomy 31:6 Be strong and courageous. Do not be afraid or terrified because of them, for the Lord your God goes with you; he will never leave you nor forsake you."*

The Holy Spirit had to help me heal my "people wounds". Those are the hurts that happen when we put so much faith in human beings that when they don't perform the way we want them to we are left hurt. We can harbor those hurts if we're not careful. I had to learn to give people the same grace card that God gave to me through His Son Jesus. I've learned to ask God what He was trying to show me about myself. I search for the good in every situation. I literally asked God to help me get past those snags. Now I can shake off those offenses. I won't say I'm never moved when people render hurt, but now I can forgive, move past it, and let it go.

There has been a series of stops, twists, and turns throughout my life because that is what life is all about. God builds us up by constructing a perfectly fit house within us where He can live. He didn't promise us a trouble-free existence, but He did promise to always be there for us.

"James 1:2-4 Consider it pure joy my brothers and sisters, whenever you face trials of many kinds, because you

know that the testing of your faith produces perseverance. Let perseverance finish its works so that you may be mature and complete, not lacking anything."

There is a reason for everything God allows. He knows at all times what He is perfecting inside of each of us. After all, we are His. The things you go through that don't feel good are as much a part of the plan as the good things that happen. Nothing is wasted. God uses it all for His glory and our good if we allow it.

We just have to trust the process. I'm many years post college now, and God is still my God. I know Him as more than my parent's God. He is my Savior and my best friend. The tests and trials only drew me closer to Him. That's what He wants…a close relationship. He will allow those tests and trials to bring us closer to Him. In the end you will always be glad that He did.

I can attest to the fact that some of the storms that I faced came directly from my choices. When we make choices that go against God's will we open the door to the enemy to slip in & wreak havoc. Remember his job is to kill, steal, and destroy. He slithers around like the snake he is trying to find cracks in our armor. So, we have to be careful that we're knowing causing storms in our lives them getting upset when it rains.

Our choices matter, even as believers. This is why it's so important to spend time in the word.

We need to know what really is right in God's eyes versus what the world says is right.

CHAPTER 4

Being a believer has nothing to do with your feelings. That first and foremost is something you need to grasp. Some days you will "feel" saved, on other days you may not. Your salvation has nothing to do with how you feel about yourself. Once you accepted Jesus as your Lord and Savior that sealed your salvation. You are saved. You are His. When God looks at you now, He sees His Son Jesus hanging on that cross for you; not the person you see in the mirror with faults and shortcomings. To God you have become perfect, because the perfect Lamb died in your place.

The enemy wants you to get caught up in your behavior. He wants your bad behavior to stick out like a sore thumb that you just accidentally hit while hammering a nail. He wants your sin throbbing constantly in your mind. If you're not careful you'll focus on the fact that you lost your temper, lied, drank that intoxicating drink, fornicated, or whatever you did that he could use against you to bring guilt, condemnation, and shame, reminding you that you missed the mark.

The fact is God no longer remembers your sin, past or present. He really wants to love you into a life that allows you to stop living like you use to live.

Colossians 1:21-22 "Once you were alienated from God and were enemies in your minds because of your evil behavior. But now he has reconciled you by Christ's physical body through death to present you holy in his sight, without blemish and free from accusation."

That's love. Although we were all wrong and living outside His will at one point, He looks past our faults to see Jesus on the cross as payment for our sin. He sees His perfect sacrifice in the Lamb Jesus Christ.

It's as if He literally throws your past into the sea of forgetfulness. He doesn't go back and dig it up when you're feeling low. He doesn't bring it up when you've messed up again and again. He just keeps on loving you. He allows the lessons to keep coming to allow you to learn and grow from them.

What makes this so special is that the Holy Spirit living inside of us is at work within us. He speaks wisdom and truth as He seeks to guide us the right way. The experiences we encounter actually help to bring us closer to dependence on Him as we see Him helping us through things that we couldn't accomplish or overcome on our own. He loves us to wholeness. He loves us into His holiness.

As believers it is literally impossible to keep living the same old life we've lived before once we are in full blown relationship with Him. Once you are saved your appetite will begin to change little by little. It is a process that we must all go through. Some people are able to immediately stop living the old way in which their flesh (carnal nature) ruled their day. For most, however, it is a process that takes time. Some people immediately stop drinking, smoking, using foul language, or whatever their vice may be. For others it takes time.

The bottom line is wherever your battle is-is an area of weakness for you. It is a realm in which your flesh has been practicing behavior that is not Christ-like. Don't feel alone. I haven't always made the best choices and I no longer bare shame about that fact. There was a lot that I didn't know. Every human being shares your journey.

There was a time in my life where I felt out of control. I wanted to change but I didn't know how to. I was locked into soul ties and didn't know it. I was heartbroken and very disappointed in myself for my weaknesses. I didn't know that the enemy operates through familiar spirits. He flows through our bad habits and behaviors, our friendships and relationships, and he uses them against us. I believe that that's why Psalm 1:1 is so important. *"Blessed is the man who walks not in the counsel of the ungodly, nor stands in the path of sinners, nor seats in the sear of the scornful; but his delight is in the law of the Lord, and in His law he meditates day and night."*

The Bible warns us to not be deceived in 1 Corinthians 15:33; "Bad company corrupts good character." It doesn't matter how sweet or innocent you start out, hanging around people who are living foul can eventually influence you and your behavior. Many people have gotten caught up thinking they could change another person and help them get it together. It does happen. There are good soul ties too, but if you're someone who's seeking to wait until marriage before having sex, for example, you cannot date someone who has had sex and expect them to not influence you to have sex. No matter how well-intended they may be, eventually they're going to try to influence you their way. The devil wouldn't be who he is if he didn't use them to influence you. It's the same thing with drugs, alcohol, & most sin.

I got locked into a cycle of guilt and condemnation because of a few choices I made when I was younger. That season of guilt and condemnation lasted many more years than it should have because there were so many things that I did not understand about how the enemy operates. I did not know that disobedience was a door to allow the enemy to work against me. But God knew. I didn't know that condemnation was a wrong feeling.

As a believer I was not supposed to feel condemned by God. That's one of the many things I love about Him. He so graciously started a process of transformation inside of me through my mistakes that He knew would in the end bear fruit of righteousness. He knew that He could take my mistakes and in turn use them to cause me to be a blessing to others. It is the same with you. Nothing you have been through will ever be wasted once you truly submit your life to Christ. He will use your testimony to bless someone else. Your sins and mistakes did not and do not disqualify you.

We are not our sins. We are not those bad things we do or have done in our flesh. We are not fornicators. We are not idolaters. We are not backbiters. We are not liars. We are not adulterers. We are not drug heads. We are not alcoholics. The bottom line is we are not what we do. We are children of the Most High God.

Once we receive Jesus as our Lord and Savior, the sacrifice for our sin, we were set free from our behavior. God begins to set us free from ourselves and our way of being. It is a process. We have to remember this because our enemy, the devil, will try to use our behavior against us. He has no power outside of what we give him. He will use whatever he can to seduce us into condemning ourselves. He wants us always looking at ourselves for our salvation, overlooking what Jesus did. That's why we have to understand **Romans 8:1** and fully accept it for ourselves, *"There is now no condemnation (no guilty verdict, no punishment) for those who are in Christ Jesus (who believe in Him as personal Lord and Savior)..."* Period, point blank, it is settled in Heaven; so, let it be settled in you.

What gets us that even though we were or are now saved we still find ourselves in the same behaviors that we know don't please God and leave us feeling terrible about ourselves. That's where the process kicks in. **Romans 12:2** admonishes us *"Do not conform to the patterns of this world, but be transformed by the renewing of your mind."*

When we find ourselves in the position of doing what we use to do we have to shake it off by praying it off of us. Otherwise, the enemy will use our own thoughts against us to discourage us. We must not only make **Romans 8:1** and part of our routine declarations, but we must make **2 Corinthians 10:5** a part of our everyday life as well. *"Casting down imaginations, and every high thing that exalteth itself against the knowledge of God, and bringing into captivity every thought to the obedience of Christ..."* We literally have to go to battle against our thoughts when they're putting us in a place of guilt, condemnation, loneliness, unworthiness, and any other unhealthy emotional head space.

Discouragement is one of the greatest weapons our enemy, the devil, tries to use against believers. The enemy especially wants to get newly converted Christians caught up in distraction. He uses guilt, condemnation, and discouragement as arrows every chance he gets. He wants us feeling low and full of doubt about who we are and Who we belong to. He loves to use your mistakes against you.

So, you have to be ready. You have to prepare your mind to be on guard when feelings of guilt and condemnation set in because they go against the word of God for believers. Again, remember the Bible says in *Romans 8:1 "There is therefore now no condemnation to those who are in Christ Jesus, who do not walk after the flesh, but according to the Spirit."* What God did was give us His Holy Spirit when we confessed our belief in Jesus as our Lord and Savior. That means Christ's spirit (essence), which is Holy, came to live and dwell within us. His spirit becomes our spiritual nature once we receive Christ as our redeemer.

When we are outside of God's will in our actions, behavior, speech, or in any area of our lives; His spirit within us convicts us. The Holy Spirit reminds us who we are and Who we belong to. He doesn't remind you how bad you. So, if you are living outside of what you know the will of God to be and you feel worthless; know that the enemy may have a foot hold on you. He's trying to keep you right where you are feeling off track and worthless. If you're feeling a strong sense of guilt and worthlessness, stand up against the enemy and begin to declare the word of God over your life. Repent of your sin (confess any sin in your life) and remind yourself that you are the righteousness of God's through faith in Christ Jesus. Then tell your enemy. Remind him that you know he is the father of lies and the author of confusion. Remind him that you know what God says about you; that you are saved and set free by the precious blood of the Lamb. Then move on.

I wish I could say that if you do this one time that you won't need to do it again, but truth is, you'll continuously be in this battle with your mortal enemy and your flesh (carnal, natural self). The devil doesn't want the children of God to believe their salvation is fixed. So, he picks his fights with our heads and hearts, always stirring up some kind of confusion.

But God is not like man. He cannot lie; there-fore, what He promised in His word shall come to pass. We can believe every word He spoke. Every word in the Bible is God breathed. He ordained His word. It is holy, and it is true.

This is why praying and knowing the word of God is so important. These two things are powerful weapons against that bully. We have been given the mind of Christ, but we must know His word in order to grasp how He thinks.

I'll never forget when I was younger, I thought everything was a sin. I grew up in a little old Baptist Church where the message of grace did not exist. So, I spent a lot of time pondering my mistakes and choices. Little did I know that I only needed to take the pressure off myself and put those burdens on Jesus Christ. The character flaws I didn't have the power to change on my own, Jesus was ready to help me break. So, I say to you, whether you're saved or not; take off those heavy weights and chains of your past and put them on Jesus. Take up His yoke. His yoke is easy, and His burdens are light. Cast every care and concern in your heart on Him. He cares for you and wants to help deal with your issues.

CHAPTER 5

You will never be perfect in this life in and of yourself so don't waste time trying to be. Instead focus on the cross of Christ and what He did hanging from the tree for you. He broke every chain, weight, and punishment that was set against you.

I was confused for many years about the things of God because my leaders didn't understand that they were teaching us to live by the law, rather than under the grace of God. They unknowingly put the focus on our behavior versus what Jesus did. I spent many years beating myself up thinking I wasn't good enough for God and His best. I would do well in one area and mess up in another, beating myself down every step of the way. Little did I know that ignorance and the devil were the culprits behind these self-defeating thoughts. It got so bad that after a while he didn't have to come after me, my flesh took a hold of these negative thoughts and I turned on myself. If you're someone who's been a Christian for any length of time you know exactly what I'm talking about.

I don't want that for those of you who are just getting to know Christ. I don't want you to spend years thinking that you have to be perfect & beating yourself down when you fall short. What I didn't fully grasp, and many don't; is that in God's love and wisdom He knew that we could not keep all of His laws. I can guarantee you will fall short thinking that you can be perfect in and of yourself. So, you have to get this straight for yourself. If you ever attempt to keep all of the written laws, you will fail. You cannot fulfill all of the laws of the Bible. No person ever has, and no one ever will. Jesus Christ did that. He handled it more than 2,000 years ago. He is the only one who ever could. *Matthew 5:17* is clear, *"Don't misunderstand why I have come. I did not come to abolish the law of Moses or the writings of the prophets. No, I came to accomplish their purpose."*

Let us be clear. The Old Testament is God's covenant with the Jewish people. It was based on the customs and laws God set in place for His people. The blood sacrifices of animals performed through priests was a part of God's relationship with His people, the Jews. You and I were Gentiles before Jesus came. We weren't factored in. There was no covenant for us. However, God in His love for us saw that no man could fulfill the law, so He sent His only Son Jesus to make the sacrifice for us all. Jesus literally walked among man to show man how to live with and through temptation without succumbing to it. God gave us

Jesus to fulfill the laws of the Old Testament because God knew the Jews couldn't and neither could we. Not one person is capable of fulfilling all of the laws. If we are right in one area and falling short in another, this means we haven't been fully obedient. So, Christ died for us doing away with the need for Old Testament Levitical priesthood sacrifices that had to be done over and over. He gave His life one time for us all forever abolishing our sin. **Hebrews 10:12-14** seals it *"But when Christ had offered for all time a single sacrifice for sins, he sat down at the right hand of God, waiting from that time until His enemies should be made and footstool for His feet. For by a single offering He has perfected for all time those who are being sanctified."*

This also means that whenever we find ourselves doing sinful things, we are the still the righteousness of God's through Christ Jesus. He finished it. So rather than giving us the punishment we deserve for disobeying the laws; like lying, cheating, coveting, judging others, and etc. what Jesus did was enough. God sent His Son Jesus who took all of our sins upon Himself when He died on the cross. It was done once for all of us because God knew that none of us could ever take on the weight of our own sin. He knew none of us would be righteous enough in ourselves to never disobey His laws.

We don't have to do anything but receive what He did on the cross for us to be saved. His Spirit then goes to work on the inside, rooting out and bringing awareness to the things and attitudes living inside of us that don't reflect His nature. You and I will never be perfect, but it's so good to know that when God looks at us, He sees His Son Jesus. He sees us sinless and set free, because His Son is perfect.

God's heart is for every Christian who has accepted Jesus as Lord and Savior to then begin to learn His nature by studying His word. Romans 12:2 says, "And do not be conformed to this world, but be transformed by the renewing of your mind, that you may prove what is that good and acceptable and perfect will of God." If a Christian immediately immerses themselves in the word of God; meaning reading the Bible, they will begin immediately changing on the inside. That is what the word of God does. It changes us from the inside out. It exposes us to God's heart toward us and His will for us as believers. It also exposes the truth of what happens for those who do not believe in Jesus.

It's also important to remember that with sin comes consequence. Sin has the ability to set things in motion. Those things are most often negative that can lead you down a wrong hurtful path. So as wonderful as having Jesus take the punishment for our sin, it does not absolve us from seeking to live right. Doing bad things carry negative consequences. So, for your own sake of peace the Bible urges us in **Philippians 4:8** to focus on the positive things. *"Finally, brother, whatever is true, whatever is honorable, whatever is just, whatever is pure, whatever is lovely, whatever is commenda-ble, if there is any excellence, if there is anything worthy of praise, think about these things."*

CHAPTER 6

rayer is a necessity for your everyday life. Prayer is simply talking to God in the name of His Son Jesus Christ. It is one of the most powerful things we can do as human beings not only for ourselves, but for others as well. God is your father and He is your friend. He created you for Himself; so that you could have access to Him. He loves you unconditionally. He wants you to tell Him everything. He wants to help you. He wants to provide for you. He wants to protect you when you feel unsafe. He wants to give you direction. He wants to give you His wisdom. He wants to fight for you. He wants to give you hope and peace. He wants to download His perfect will and plan for your life into your mind and spirit. But this type of intimacy comes through a relationship with Him. Just as communication is important in our relationships with family and friends, coworkers, and any other human being, so it is with our relationship with God through His Son Jesus Christ.

Prayer is an opportunity to talk to God sharing your thoughts, wishes, and dreams. Prayer allows you to reveal your hurts, pains, struggles in the presence of the only one who could never hurt you with your own words and thoughts. In His presence there's no judgment only love and clear direction.

Praying gives you the chance to connect directly to God like plugging the power cord of a lamp into the wall. Once the cord is plugged into the outlet the light comes on. In turn when you pray you plug into God and your light comes on. The light of your heart connected to His heart is a safe place. He reveals His heart to us as we plug in to Him. Even when we do things that don't please Him, and we feel unplugged, His outlet is still there. Prayer plugs you right back in and allows you to talk to God and confess to Him those things that break His heart and keep you up at night.

Prayer allows you to release those things, so you won't go around feeling bad inside. God doesn't want His children feeling badly about themselves. That's why rather than condemning yourself and feeling guilty, He allows us to open up and confess our wrongs, so He can remind us that He loves us. His Spirit within us reminds us that His Son Jesus Christ died for our sins, so we don't have to wallow in the bad feelings that sin produces separating us from God. Instead, you can repent before Him which means you confess your sin to God then turn away from the sin behavior, so you can keep on living for Christ.

At the end of these chapters I have written a list of prayers & affirmations that are only meant to be a guide in helping you begin your prayer journey. Don't forget to ask the Holy Spirit to lead you in prayer. He knows us better than we know ourselves. He will guide you because He knows you. I must remind you that there will be times when, "Lord, help me" will be the strongest prayer you will ever pray. You can rest assured that He will be there to help you.

CHAPTER 7

Don't leave the Holy Spirit out. You should pray because you need to know the truth about God. You also need to know the truth about the devil. According to the word in John 10:10 "*The thief (the devil) comes only to steal, kill, and destroy, I (Jesus) have come that they may have life, and have it to the full.*"

That means our enemy is on the prowl. He and his minions are always seeking those they can devour. Not literally, but in the spiritual sense. Their job is to snatch every bit of belief out of believers rendering them powerless to stand. If you don't know the power that is working on the inside of you their job becomes easier. Don't let this scare you. Because of God's grace we are not powerless. We are not left without a leg to stand on. In John 16:7 Before Jesus went to the cross, He had a conversation with His disciples letting them know that His departure was at hand. He was assuring them that He wasn't leaving them by themselves. He told them that He would be sending the Holy Spirit after His departure. "But I tell you the truth, it is to your advantage that I go away; for if I do not go away, the Helper (Comforter, Advocate, Intercessor, Counselor, Strengthener, Standby) will not come to you; but if I go, I will send Him (The Holy Spirit) to you (to be in close fellowship with you).

As I said previously, He did not just send the Holy Spirit to hover around us. He sent His own spirit to live inside of us. **John 16:13-15** *"But when he, the Spirit of truth, comes, he will guide you into all the truth. He will not speak on his own; he will speak only what he hears, and he will tell you what is yet to come. He will glorify me because it is from me that he will receive what he will make known to you. All that belongs to the Father is mine. That is why I said the Spirit will receive from me what he will make known to you."*

There are so many choices to make in a lifetime. We are all faced with choices on a daily basis. Whether you're ten years old, twenty-five, or sixty-five reading this book that will be true. Your decisions can make life hard or easy for you. God knew this when He sent His spirit. He knew that on our own we would have no clue what we are doing on this earth. So, He impregnated all believers with His Spirit, which means His wisdom, strength, truth, temperament, love, and His power are in us.

We, however, must make sure we don't allow the Holy Spirit to lie dormant within us. We have to on purpose ask Him to help us. We have to acknowledge God in all things and ask the Holy

Spirit to literally lead us and guide us in the way we should go.

Sadly, some of the situations we are faced with in life can be confusing. They will sometimes appear one way or to be one thing but might actually be something different altogether. We sometimes have to ask God's Holy Spirit within us what we are looking at and to help us see it clearly. You will need to pray and talk to Him about the decisions you make. You will need to know His will when you choose what to do.

Knowing His will comes through prayer and reading the Bible. Unfortunately, the devil is our mortal enemy. He wants to kill, steal, and destroy all of our lives because he is jealous of the children of God. He made the fatal mistake of wanting to be God; and he lost all access, rights, and privileges to God, the things of God, and Heaven. This makes him angry because instead of having power over us, God gave us power over him. *Luke 10:19 says "God has given us authority to trample on snakes and scorpions and over all the power of the enemy, therefore, nothing shall by any means harm us."*

The enemy has no real power except that we give him by living a life of sin. Understand that the enemy is a manifestation of every evil thing. He is a like a magnet drawing all negativity to himself. Anger, jealousy, hate, fear, bitterness, racism, sexism, rage, robbing, stealing, killing and every evil work is in his realm and are, therefore, under his sphere of influence. So, we have to pray and ask God to help us to discern when we are teetering and tottering outside of His will. We have to ask Him to help us to stay away from those things that could do us harm and cause us to go back to that old life which gained us nothing. *James 4:7* says *"Resist the devil and he will flee from you"*. So, resist him when he comes for you because he is coming. It's his nature.

You can't do it alone. You need a safe place to go with your problems. You need to feel safe knowing you can trust and depend on God. You need to know that you are loved unconditionally. Having a relationship with Him and allowing Him to lead is the only way to truly know His heart and just how deeply He does love you. The word says in **Isaiah 26:3** *"You will keep him in perfect peace, whose mind is stayed on You, because he trusts in You."*

There is comfort in talking to Him all the time. On the days that you don't feel so good about yourself you'll feel safe asking the Holy Spirit to help you. Turning to God in prayer to help you deal with those feelings will always bring a sense of peace.

CHAPTER 8

Your mess ups don't disqualify you. As surely as you live those days will come where you feel lousy because oops you did it again. If they haven't already come, they will. You will make a wrong choice or two or three at some point. Bad decisions can sometimes leave you feeling and thinking negatively about yourself and your future. Bad decisions can even make you feel God doesn't love you anymore and that you're unworthy of being loved. Condemnation leaves you believing you've messed up so badly that God can't forgive you. So, you find it hard to forgive yourself.

But because you have a relationship with God His spirit will comfort you and remind you that in spite of your mistakes you are still loved and forgiven. You still belong to God and that He always wants you to move forward. The Bible says that where sin abounds grace abounds much more.

Relationship with God through His Spirit and praying opens your spiritual ears to hear what God is saying to you. It is how we go deeper in our relationship with Him.

Believers need to learn as early as possible in life to pray to God about everything and to ask the Holy Spirit for help. The earlier we learn how to pray and use the leading of the Holy Spirit the stronger we will become.

I believe one of the greatest sources of weakness we experience as believers is not knowing that the power of God lives in us. This power isn't some mystical thing. It is literally God's power. It is the same power that raised Jesus Christ from the dead after He was buried. Jesus was literally dead after having gone to the cross with every force of evil energy in Him. This power broke through all of that evil and eradicated all sin forever. Now that is power. The amazing truth is that power lives in you and me. We have to accept this truth and we have to nurture our relationship with the Holy Spirit to actively involve Him in our lives. It's not in God's nature to force us to do anything. His Spirit nudges us, and gives us righteous thoughts, but He will not force our hands when He's given us free will.

We need to be free to tell God everything. Adults and children, alike, should talk to Him about our families. You should tell him about your friends and ask Him to guide us in our friendships. Whether you're a young person or an adult you have to talk to Him about the steps you are taking every day. You should ask if you should get into the vehicle with your friends after the game and if you should go to the party at your friend's house whose parents are out of town. You can ask Him if you should ask your parents for those hot new shoes or wait. You should seek Him about that new job you're interviewing for. You should ask Him if the person you are considering dating is someone He approves of. You should ask Him for help with your studies and tests.

If you're an adult, you should ask Him if you're making the right decision marrying someone. You should ask Him if you should buy the new dress or loan the money to your sister for her bills. You should talk to Him about your investments of money and time. You can ask Him about that situation at work that's bothering you. You seek His wisdom by asking if you should say something to that boss who's really making you feel uncomfortable, and if so, what to say and how to say it safely. Sometimes He urges us to just be still while He fights those situations for us.

God is the author of clarity. He's not the author of confusion. So, if there's a place in your life that is confused; talk to God about it. In *Psalm 138:8* God promised to perfect those things that concern us. *"The Lord will perfect that which concerns me; Your mercy, O Lord, endures forever"*

CHAPTER 9

Read the Bible every day. This is the most important part of your day. It's like what happens when the old cartoon character Popeye would eat His spinach. He got power. Seriously, the word of God is really like that when believers read it. We are filled with the power of God through His word because it opens us up to a deeper revelation of God than sitting in church hearing a man teach the word. Reading the Bible is a direct connection to God's spirit. He downloads directly from His Spirit into ours through His word.

As you go through your life you will need to know His truth in order to clearly understand the things that are happening around you and to you. You will need to understand why. The Bible is God's truth. He left us with His word because He wanted us to get to know Him and who we are in Him. He also knew we would need our weapons. The Bible is a weapon against the enemy just like praying. Knowing the word of God can help believers tear the devil's playhouse down. Knowing the word helps us to take a stand on God's promises in the Bible. That's His will for us. There are over five thousand promises of God in the Bible for His children. If you never open the Bible you won't know what those promises are.

Studying the word is no different from the study habits developed in school. The earlier you set study habits in school the better you are at studying and the better you perform in school. It's the same principle with reading the Bible. The earlier you learn to study the word the stronger you'll become in your everyday life. The more you study the word the more you're able to accomplish the purposes and plans of God for your life.

You take in what you put in. If you put in a lot of time studying His word and talking to Him; you'll learn more and more about Him and His promises for your life. The more you digest His words the more you'll learn of the power He put inside of you. You'll hear His voice and walk in this power. You can truly be a weapon against darkness when you know who you are in Him.

CHAPTER 10

Get *Rid of the Confusion.* As an adult I realized there are so many things that I was taught as a little girl that just don't line up with the word of God. First, the notion that we have to be cleaned up before giving our lives to Christ is a lie. God wants us to come to Him as we are right now, so He can clean us up. Only He can cleanse us.

Being saved has absolutely nothing to do with how you dress, where you live, what you eat, how many hours you spend praying, how bad you use to be. So, don't allow any of these things to make you think otherwise. Don't allow what people think or say to infiltrate your thoughts about your salvation. If the word of God says you're saved, you are saved.

The Bible tells us to pray all the time. Most of us were taught to pray before going to bed at night and when we rise in the morning. However, praying is our open communication with God; and He is always listening. So that means you can pray to Him anytime, anywhere, any way.

You can talk to God while riding in the car. You can pray while walking down the street. You can pray when you're happy telling God thank You. Pray in the shower. You can pray in your own personal War Room or private spot you set aside for prayer if you want. It doesn't matter where you pray. It only matters that you pray.

The great thing about prayer is that you can literally tell God everything and never have to worry about Him telling someone else. He already knows your heart. There is no secret feeling that we have that He doesn't already know about. So, there is no judgment.

You can talk to Him without opening your mouth. It can be an inward prayer in your mind or spoken prayer. Sometimes in life situations will call for inward prayer, but because of the setting may not allow for you to take a knee to pray.

Again, God is for you and He will always be there for you. He is on your side. He wants only the best for your life. Whether you are in a good situation or one that's not ideal; God's plans for your life are for good.

As an adult I realized there are so many things that I was taught as a little girl that just don't line up with the word of God. First, the notion that we have to be cleaned up before giving our lives to Christ is a lie. God wants us to come to Him as we are right now, so He can clean us up. Only He can cleanse us.

You don't have to do any certain thing any certain way that puts your salvation on you. We only need to accept what Jesus did on the cross. You can't perform in a way that gains you salvation. Jesus' death, burial, and resurrection alone is our access into the divine life of Christ and the kingdom of God. So, connect with God whenever you feel like it. Show us just as you are without fear of rejection. Talk to Him about whatever you feel you need to talk to Him about. Pray even when you don't feel like it. Talk to Him, especially when you don't feel like it.

CHAPTER 11

Don't stress out about anything, instead talk to God. *Philippians 4:6-7 "Be anxious for nothing, but in everything by prayer and supplication, with thanksgiving, let your requests be made known to God; and the peace of God, which surpasses all understanding, will guard your hearts and minds through Christ Jesus."*

God really is our Father. He wants us to depend on Him. He wants us to do so with ease. So, you going to Him over and over is what He wants. He wants to hear our wants and even what we think we need. He wants us to come thanking Him for what He's done, doing, and for what He is going to do. He doesn't want us doing things on your own. He wants you and I to turn to Him.

Contrary to what people may say, what the whispers of the enemy may sound like, and no matter what your own flesh may say; God never gets tired of His children coming to Him and leaning on Him to meet our needs. It doesn't stress Him out. It only stresses us out when we try to do life on our own. We're up the creek without a paddle without God leading us. So, we have to go to Him. When we stress, we can't hear Him.

So, we can't follow Him in a way that's effective. So, let go of the stressing and grab onto the blessing He laid out in Philippians 4:6.

You can talk to Him as Savior and Lord, friend, comforter, healer, provider, lover, redeemer, doctor, restorer, and so many forms of Himself. He is able to meet you at your point of need. So, if you have a problem look in the Bible and find scriptures that speak to your problem. Pray God's word back to Him. Thank Him. Make your requests to Him. He is obligated to keep His word. Isaiah 55:11 *"So shall my word be that goes forth from My mouth: it shall not return to Me void, But it shall accomplish what I please, And it shall prosper in the thing for which I sent it."*

He promises us His peace when we do what He says for us to do. Trust Him. Trust His word. Don't keep going in circles wandering around trying to figure it all out on your own. Let Philippians 4:6 be your guide.

CHAPTER 12

You must forgive those who hurt you. This is as much for you as it is for them. Holding back forgiveness works on the inside of you the person who won't forgive. It goes against who you were created to be. It operates negatively against your health, your thinking, and your ability to accomplish anything worthwhile. It can be seen on your face and in how you treat others. It tightens you up like a fist. Is this how you want to live? Of course, not so forgive. *Mark 11:24-25 New International Version* *"Therefore I tell you, whatever you ask for in prayer, believe that you have received it, and it will be yours. And when you stand praying, if you hold anything against anyone, forgive them, so that your Father in heaven may forgive you your sins."*

The reason God tells us to forgive is because He knows that not forgiving can be a blessing blocker and it also opens the door to the enemy to operate in a believer's life. He doesn't want us holding on to anything that would keep us from His blessings.

Instead of getting into offense let the hurts remind you that we've also been forgiven much ourselves. When I think about how many times I've broken God's heart living beneath His privilege and standards for my life; doing things I never thought I would do, I'm ashamed. Then I remember He tells me to remember no more the shame of my past because I don't live there anymore. I remember that as dirty and as spotted up as I've been at points in my life, He never once failed to wash me and make me whole again. He cleansed me from all unrighteousness when I asked Him to forgive me and make me whiter than snow. He has always restored me.

He has the full expectation of us showing this type of grace to those who offend us. He wants us to set our souls free in the process of releasing others.

CHAPTER 13

Life won't be perfect because you're saved or stop the enemy's attacks or keep bad things from happening. This reality check is one that a lot of believers and new believers need to understand. The Bible is clear. In fact, scripture says in *Matthew 5:44-46 "But I tell you, love your enemies and pray for those who persecute you, that you may be children of your Father in heaven. He causes His sun to rise on the evil and the good and sends rain on the righteous and the unrighteous. If you love those who love you, what reward will you get? Are not even the tax collectors doing that?"*

So, as you can see this scripture is so prolific in its truth that God strategically placed it in the middle of telling us to love people, including our enemies. God created us, and he knows the hearts and minds of the people He created. That means He already knew that we would be mistreated, used, and perhaps abused at times by people. He also knew that sometimes no matter how good you're trying to be to others, they may not receive it the way you want. So, He lets us know we should expect it and be prepared to meet people with love in spite of how they may treat us.

He also knows that the enemy wants to take us all out. If he could satan would wipe us all out. Good news is he can't. But what he does do is attempt to impact our lives with his many arrows of wickedness, lies, deceptions, manipulation, illnesses, and etc. He brings with him lying spirits, cheating spirits, sickness, fear, dishonesty, and so many other things that if manifested causes trials and tribulations for people.

As believers we can't just shut down when the enemy comes after us and our families. We have to use the power in the blood of Jesus and plead it over ourselves, our family, our homes, our jobs, and everything that concerns us. **Revelation 12:11***says "And they have conquered him by the blood of the Lamb and by the word of their testimony, for they loved not their lives even unto death."*

We overcome the devil by the blood of Jesus and by telling what God had done for us. How He brought us out of the dark places and delivered us.

I want to share a truth that if you can grasp right now will give you another level of freedom as a new believer.

If God allows you to encounter a problem, troubles, or a set of circumstances; He already built a way of escape through His Son Jesus. In other words, if God brought you to it, He'll guide you through it. It may not be easy. But the enemy has no new tricks. The things he's doing now he was doing when he fell from heaven as a fallen angel. God has given us the manual to step on his head. Our weapons are written all over and throughout the Bible. But we must go after them. We have to open up our Bibles and read what God says about the matter, and we must ask Him to help us. It doesn't matter how good you are. If you don't know your power; you're powerless.

I wish it were that because we believe in God that bad things would cease. One day they will, but as long as we have an enemy who is "like" a roaring lion roaming this earth seeking people to devour; we have to fight. We were all put on this earth with a divine destiny, a plan that God set in motion before we were ever born. If we don't seek Him and His will, we won't reach that place. If we don't fight for what belongs to us dreams will die. Graveyards are full of untapped potential, purpose, and promise.

There are so many people struggling with financial problems, broken marriages, sicknesses, broken hearts, and so many things that life brings. They're going through because they're not fighting back and they're not learning the word and growing in it. We were made to withstand whatever life brings. We were made to walk in victory. Many people have found a sense of comfort in wallowing in their present situations. Instead of settling for a life less than the one you desire fight for your inheritance. Get in the word and learn what God's promises are to those who believe. Then use that word. Speak it out loud into the atmosphere where the enemy hears. Don't lose hope based on what you're looking at. You're not going through anything that others haven't. In fact, James wrote in *James 1:2-4 says "Consider it pure joy, my brothers and sisters, whenever you face trials of many kinds, because you know that the testing of your faith produces perseverance. Let perseverance finish its work so that you may be mature and complete, not lacking anything."*

So, fight! You have all the tools you need. Plead the blood of Jesus and the word of God. Every time an attack comes you have to remind the enemy that *"No weapon formed against you shall prosper, And every tongue which rises against you in judgment you shall condemn. This is the heritage of the servants of the Lord, and their righteousness is from Me,"* Says the Lord.

We cannot sit on our hands hoping and wishing the enemy would leave us alone. We have to fight back with the forces of Heaven. The enemy's assaults are real. So, we must be even more so in our own full-blown counter attack on the enemy's plans. **Ephesians 6:10-18 Finally**, *my brethren, be strong in the Lord and in the power of His might. Put on the whole armor of God that you may be able to stand against the wiles of the devil. For we do not wrestle against flesh and blood, but against principalities, against powers,* *against the rulers of the darkness of this age, and against spiritual hosts of wickedness in the heavenly places. Therefore take up the whole armor of God, that you may be able to withstand in the evil day, and having done all, to stand, Stand therefore, having girded your waist with truth, having put on the breastplate of righteousness, and having shod your feet with the preparation of the gospel of peace; above all, taking the shield of faith with which you will be able to quench all the fiery darts of the wicked one. And take the helmet of salvation, and the sword of the Spirit, which is the word of God; praying always with all prayer and supplication in the Spirit, being watchful to this end with all perseverance and supplication for all the saints.*

The bottom line is we have to keep going when bad things happen, keeping in mind that bad things can happen to us all. If we can remember that we were meant to endure hardships, we will win. God already won the battle for us through the death, burial, and resurrection of His Son Jesus. We just have to receive what Jesus did and use the weapons we've been given in God's word. Endure so that you will receive your crown. *James 1:12 "God bless those who patiently endure testing and temptation. Afterward they will receive the crown of life that God has promised to those who love Him."*

Also, be mindful of the fact that a lot of the problems, situations, and tests you will go through will have another human being on the other side of them. People will test you. In fact, people you care about will often be set against you. Sadly, the enemy is great at offering negative suggestions to all of us and sometimes people don't make choices that honor God or bonds with you.

It is so easy to react and get them off your back, and to get them back for wronging you in whatever way. Snap, crackle, and pop is the way today. All of us have been guilty of it at some point in our walk along this journey. The question is was it really easy after the over reaction? Going off always has negative consequences, and payback, even more so. Not to mention the fact that none of this reflects who we are as children of God. I guarantee that after you've gone off on someone or handled the situation improperly; guilt sets in. Or when you've hurt someone who has hurt you, it didn't feel good to hurt them after the dust settled. This is because we are meant to operate in love at all times. We are meant to handle situations and the people we care about and encounter with the love of Christ. That is who we are and that is why we are here. We are meant to be a reflection of His love for us in the earth.

So, the next time you do something good for someone and they don't express thanks, don't get mad. Keep doing good by them. The next time your spouse hurts your feelings, instead of hurting them back; respond with all the love and kindness you can muster up. The next time your child does something they knew better than doing, instead of yelling at them talk to them in love. The next time that boss comes to you in a demeaning way, making you feel small; stand tall and respond with love and kindness and remind yourself who you are representing in that moment. By doing so you'll be rendering up to others one of the greatest gifts God has given to you, the gift of mercy; which is the compassion or forgiveness shown toward someone when it is within one's power to punish or harm.

According to the Bible God gives us new mercy every day, along with His grace; the free and unmerited favor of God, as manifested in the salvation of sinners and the bestowal of blessings. So, we must open our hearts to give what we've been given. Unlike the way the world thinks now, this is not weakness. Anyone can be selfish, mean, unkind, harsh, and hard; but it takes something special on the inside to be so full of love that we are able to render to others the same grace and mercy that we've been given. Contrary to this world's view, meekness is not weakness. Being humble, teachable, and patient under suffering are attributes of Christ. Remember His journey to the cross? He was falsely accused, slapped, spit on, beaten and nearly torn apart for our sin which stood against Him. Then He was ultimately nailed to a tree for you and me, for crimes He did not commit. Does that sound weak to you? I don't think so. That is what meekness is. Jesus was grace under fire. So, where's the glory in that you ask? Well, think about it. After He endured all of that suffering, even going down into the pit of hell and snatching the keys of death from satan; He arose, as The Almighty King of kings, and He went to sit next to God as our Savior and our Lord. It gives me chills to think about it. I can't really perceive in my mind what all of this looked like in the spiritual realm. In as much as I love period movies of honor, like "300", Gladiator, and the like; I know they pale in comparison to this moment in time.

He endured, even though He didn't have to. He could've quit on us. Yet, He chose to keep going instead. In spite of the fact that He was going into the most painful, most heartbreaking, deepest mistreatment, ugliest accusations, ever known to any man; He still offered up these humble words to His Father, "Nevertheless, not my will, but Thy will be done". He could've stopped it all, but His love for us compelled Him to stay there hanging on that lonely loveless cross.

I promise there is a reward for this. **Galatians 6:9** puts it so plainly *"Let us not become weary in doing good, for at the proper time we will reap a harvest if we do not give up"*.

So, keep going. When you're being mistreated by a boss, co-worker, spouse, or anyone; when you put the matters in God's hands, He will make things right in the end. Your idea of right and His idea may be different, but it will work for His glory and the good of His children in the end if you allow Him to lead you.

I will never forget a News Director I once had who hired me because the station was having issues with discrimination. They were being forced to hire an African American because of the turn-over of people of color at the station. Even though the EEOC was involved it didn't stop because of the allegations that were already raised against him, which I believe was God's loving way of warning him to change his ways. When I got there it was a very tense environment. He'd set a very negative tone that carried over into the news-room. He took up his bullying tactics with me. He was very mean and condescending, almost knocking me down one day walking past me after tearing me down after one of his unconstructive critiques. I didn't try to fight back with words. I just continued to pray. I remember one day picking up my Bible and reading some of the Psalms where David spoke to God about his fierce enemies. *Psalm 35:1-2 "Contend, o Lord, with those who contend with me; Fight against those who fight against me. Take hold of buckler and shield. And rise up for my help.*

I also turned to Psalm 59:1 "Deliver me from my enemies, O my God; protect me from those who rise against me; deliver me from those who work evil and save me from those who are after my blood."

The book of Psalms is full of chapters that reference the fight against our enemy. The only true enemy we have is the devil and the tactics he uses against us that he sends in the form of spirits. Many times, people operate under these spirits and aren't aware that they've allowed themselves to be used to hurt someone else. This is what is meant in Ephesians 6:12 "For our struggle is not against flesh and blood, but against the rulers, against the authorities, against the powers of this dark world and against the spiritual forces of evil in the heavenly realms." So, we have to be mindful when we take the actions of others personally. I prayed that God would make even my enemies to be at peace with me and to help me to grasp that when people inflict pain and drama that they're usually dealing with underlying issues that have nothing to do with me.

Out of that the News Director stressed himself into sickness. You could see it before it happened because he was battling weight issues and always scowling and sweating with anger. He ended up in the hospital for a while. On his return, I'll never forget going in and checking on him telling him I'd been praying for him. For the first time since I'd met him, I saw something in his eyes that I'd never seen before; softness and peace. We sat there that day and talked like friends. I think his ordeal made him realize what was important and what to let go of.

Good things and bad things happen to us all. So, the next time you go through something or you hear of someone else going through something, don't judge their situation. Sometimes life is just happening the way the word of God said it would. You just make sure you're fully suited for the battle with the word of truth, knowing Who God Is, what His Son Jesus did for you and that you've accepted it as the finished work of your salvation; that you know God's word, that you're full of the peace of God. These Ephesians 6 articles are the suit of armor we believers wear, along with faith; that allow us to extinguish all the flaming arrows of the evil one. This is how we fight victoriously through whatever we go through. We were built to last. We were built to overcome the enemy by the Blood of the Lamb and by the words of our testimony according to Revelation 12:11.

What you're going through is nothing new. What we see happening in the world has happened before. So, don't be consumed by what it looks like in this life. *Ecclesiastes 9:11 I have seen something else under the sun: The race is not given to the swift or the battle to the strong, nor does food come to the wise or wealth to the brilliant or favor to the learned; but time and chance happen to them all.*

Make sure you know how to choose your battles in life. This is so important because not all battles are yours to fight or worth the fight. Discern through prayer and the word of God on what moves to make about your life if you should move at all.

CHAPTER 14

Let God heal your wounded soul. This may be one of the most important things to do after becoming a believer. A wounded soul can block blessings, keep you stuck, foster confusion and even make you sick. Sadly no one escapes being hurt. This is a very real thing. Soul wounds are those things that happen usually in childhood and beyond that stay with us until we go through the process of healing. Rape, divorce, incest, racism, rejection, poverty, hunger, jealousy, adultery, abuse, fornication, and disobedience, are all ways a person's soul can be wounded. When any of these spirits happen to someone especially children the wounds can go deeply into our very soul and they stay there unless we focus on the healing of our souls. These acts are where bitterness, resentment, jealousy, envy, rage, racism, violence and other wrong attitudes spring from.

James 4:1-2 says the fights, quarrels, strife, and other issues we have begin within us. *"What leads to quarrels and conflicts among you? Do they not come from your desires that wage war in your members? You are jealous and covet and your lust goes unfulfilled so you murder. You are envious and cannot obtain; so you fight*

and battle. You do not have because you do not ask."
James goes on to say that when you do ask you ask
with wrong motives.

In this day and age, it's so easy to look the lives
of others and compare our today with what other
people's lives appear to be. No one's life is as
perfect as it appears to be. Every single human
being has something they're dealing with or learning or enduring. Every single one of us has a
journey that is ours alone.

This journey will be up and down, we'll take
wins and losses, we'll be loved and undesired, we'll
struggle, we'll laugh, we'll cry, we'll be used and
abused, we'll be admired and inspired, and even
despised; we all experience life at different levels
and at our appointed times. What determines
whether we rise above what we go through and
finish our race is how we show up to meet what
life throws at us.

Galatians 5:7-10 *"You were running a good race.
Who cut in on you to keep you from obeying the truth?
That kind of persuasion does not come from the one who
calls you. "A little yeast works through the whole batch of
dough." I am confident in the Lord that you will take no
other view. The one who is throwing you into confusion,
whoever that may be, will have to pay the penalty."*

This verse is clear. We all have a race to run
that was set in motion when we were born.

God knew us before He created us in this earthly realm of time. 2 Peter 1:3 *"By his divine power, God has given us everything we need for living a godly life. We have received all of this by coming to know him, the one who called us to himself by means of his marvelous glory and excellence."*

There is nothing about us that's surprising to God. He knew everything we'd do and go through. He placed His power in us after we accepted Jesus as our Lord. We all have a greater work to do in this world. God knows that healing in our souls brings deliverance that breaks through addictions, anger, bitterness, resentment, sin, thievery, murder, toxic relationships, soul ties, and etc.

You see, until we go deep and allow the Holy Spirit to heal those places we'll always be dealing with the past on some level. Guilt and condemnation come along with soul wounds. This allows the enemy to pick at the scab of our wounds and at the right time when we're weak and vulnerable he'll re-open that wound causing us to bleed again for the thousandth time.

Instead of scabbing over our wounds and mistakes, there comes a point where we must face down the soul wounds that sometimes debilitate us causing us to shut down when we should be moving forward in victory. Jesus won it all for us dying on the cross at Calvary.

We have to accept this truth into our souls. Everything Jesus endured for us also healed us. We have to walk in that healing.

We have to start by asking the Holy Spirit to help us. Ask Him to open up the chambers and doors of our hearts and souls that we'd shut down to and heal us. Pleading the blood of Jesus over those hurts and wounds inflicted on us by others and those we committed against ourselves. We can plead the dunamis (dynamic) power of the resurrection over those wounds and over our hearts and souls. Get into the word and look for healing scriptures on healing. Everything we need to heal and break the enemy's strong holds over our lives are in the word and within us through the Holy Spirit.

We can't keep dragging around the pains of yesterday. God wants us free inside and outside living our best lives. It's all about choices and how we choose to navigate through the journey. We were created to be warriors for Christ, not worriers. Think about it this way. If God knew us before we were ever a thought in our mothers' minds, He really knows us. It means He also knows our journeys. He knows the end before the beginning. He created every one of us to win. He equipped us for winning. He doesn't want anything we've been through to break us. In fact, He allowed what we go through because He knows what He put in us; His very own spirit. So, no matter what we've gone through us to this point we can now choose to allow the Spirit of the Living God within us to lead us away from the past into the fullness of life and joy in Christ Jesus.

Prayers & Affirmations

Affirmations: *Speak to yourself and about yourself like you would speak to and about someone that you love.*

I think one of the best ways to firm up your spiritual life is through affirmations.

An affirmation is the action or process of affirming something or being affirmed, declaring or proclaiming something. It can be emotional support or encouragement according to Webster's dictionary. To affirm something is to basically speak life to it, whether good or bad. Since your words pack a lot of power, speak good things over your life. The power of life and death are in your tongue. So, if you want the best life. Speak life into your life and situations. The best place to start is in the word of God. Speak what God says.

Did you know that you can take the scriptures and place yourself in them? For instance, *Jeremiah 29:11* says *"For I know the plans I have for you, plans to prosper, not harm you; plans to give you a hope and a future."* You can take those words and affirm yourself saying, *"God's plans for me are to prosper me and not to bring me harm, His plans for me are to give me hope and a future."*

This is power. Your words are a force against the devil and his tricks and schemes. You literally have the power to stop him in his tracks simply by speaking the word of God to your situation and to him. The enemy has no choice but to stand down when it comes to the word.

You have to believe what you speak, but you must not be afraid to speak God's words over your life.

Here's a list that you can use to help you begin. When you start to feel comfortable affirming yourself you can move forward adding scriptures to these, so you can combat the flaming arrows of the devil. Also, remember, sometimes the best prayer to pray is simply "Help me, Lord".

Scripture: *"But you are a chosen people, a royal priesthood, a holy nation, God's special possession, that you may declare the praises of him who called you out of darkness into his wonderful light." 1 Peter 2:9 New International Version*

Affirmation: I am chosen by God. I belong to a royal priesthood. I am God's special possession and I declare the praises of Him who called me out of darkness into His wonderful light.

Scripture: *"You are the light of the world. A town built on a hill cannot be hidden. Matthew 5:14*

Affirmation: I am the light of the world.

Scripture: *"In him we have redemption through his blood, the forgiveness of sins, in accordance with the riches of God's grace".* Ephesians 1:7
Affirmation: I am redeemed by the blood of Jesus. All my sins are forgiven.

Scripture: *"But he was wounded for our transgressions, he was bruised for our iniquities; the punishment that brought us peace was on him, and by his wounds we are healed."* Isaiah 53:5
Affirmation: With Jesus' stripes I was healed; therefore, I give no place to sickness or disease.

Scripture: *"Christ redeemed us from the curse of the law, by becoming a curse for us: for it is written, cursed is every one that hangs on a tree."* Galatians 3:13
Affirmation: I am redeemed from the curse of the law by the blood of Jesus; therefore, I am free from sin and iniquity, poverty, & sickness.

Scripture: *"Delight yourself in the Lord, and He will give you the desires of your heart."* Psalm 37:4
Affirmation: I delight myself in the Lord and He will give me the desires of my heart.

Scripture: *"Commit your way to the Lord; trust in him, and he will act. He will bring forth your righteousness as the light, and your justice as the noonday."* Psalm 37:5-6

Affirmation: I commit my way to the Lord. I trust Him and will act. He will bring forth His righteousness as the light, and your justice as the noonday.

Scripture: *"Be still before the Lord and wait patiently for him; fret not yourself over the one who prospers in his way, over the man who carries out evil devices." Psalm 37:7*
Affirmation: I will be still before the Lord. I will wait patiently for Him. I will not fret over people who prosper in their evil ways.

Scripture: *"Who has known the mind of the Lord so as to instruct him?" But we have the mind of Christ.* 1 Corinthians 2:16
Affirmations: I have the mind of Christ; therefore, I think the way He thinks.

Scripture: *"Submit yourselves therefore to God. Resist the devil, and he will flee from you."* James 4:7
Affirmation: I submit myself to God. I resist the devil and he flees from me.

Scriptures: *"Casting down imaginations, and every high thing that exalts itself against the knowledge of God and bringing into captivity every thought to the obedience of Christ."* 2 Corinthians 10:4-6
Affirmations: I cast down imaginations and every high thing that exalts itself against the knowledge

of God and I bring into captivity every thought to the obedience of Christ.

Scripture: *"Behold, I give unto you power to tread on snakes and scorpions, and over all the power of the enemy; and nothing shall by any means hurt you."* Luke 10:19
Affirmation: God has given me the authority to tread on snakes and scorpions and over all the power of the enemy; and nothing shall by any means hurt me.

Scripture: *"For the Lord God is a sun and shield: the Lord will give grace, favor, and glory! No good thing will He withhold from them that walk uprightly."* Psalms 84:11
Affirmations: The Lord is a sun and my shield. The Lord has given me grace, favor, and glory. No good thing will He withhold from me because I walk uprightly through Christ.

Scriptures: *"But my God will supply all your needs according to His riches in glory by Christ Jesus."* Psalm 4:19
Affirmations: My God will supply all of my needs according to His riches in glory by Christ Jesus. Psalm 4:19

Scriptures: *"Let them say continually, Let the Lord be magnified, Who takes pleasure in the prosperity of His servant."* Psalms 35:27

Affirmation: The Lord takes pleasure in my prosperity.

Scripture: *"He set himself to seek God in the days of Zechariah, who instructed him in the things of God. As long as he sought the Lord, God made him prosper."* 2 Chronicles 26:5

Affirmations: As long as I seek the Lord, God will cause me to prosper.

Scripture: *"Humble yourselves therefore under the mighty hand of God, that He may exalt you in due time. Cast all your cares on Him for He cares for you."* 1 Peter 5:7

Affirmation: I humble myself under God's almighty hand. In due time, He will lift me up. I cast all of my concerns on Him for He cares for me.

Scripture: *"For I am not ashamed of the Gospel of Jesus Christ, for it is the power of God unto salvation to everyone that believeth."* Romans 1:16

Affirmation: I am not ashamed of the Gospel of Jesus, for it is the power of God unto my salvation as a believer.

Prayer for Family & Friends

Dear Heavenly Father, I come to you in the name of your Son Jesus Christ. I come to you with a heart of repentance for any sin that may be hindering our fellowship. Lord, I ask that you cover and protect me, my family, my friends, coworkers, church members, teachers, _____, _____, and _____. Father, I ask for the divine protection of your angels. Lord, encamp your angels around me and everyone I have prayed for today. In Jesus' name, I ask that your angels drive out and force out any demonic spirit that may try to come against us. I plead the blood of Jesus over myself and everyone I have prayed for. Cover us everywhere we go and guard us from the enemy. Lord, I thank you for answering my prayer. In Jesus Name, I pray, Amen.

Prayer for When the Enemy Attacks

Dear Heavenly Father, I come to You in Your Son Jesus' name. Lord, I'm asking for Your divine protection against the plots and plans of the enemy. According to Your word Psalm 91 I abide under Your shadow as your child. You are my refuge and my strength. I lean and rely on you. Because of Your word, I will not fear the terrors, arrows, pestilences, or destruction sent by the enemy to cause me to fear or quit. I thank You that Your angels are encamped around me protecting me from all hurt, harm, and danger. Lord, I ask that You cause Your angels to protect me from dangers that I can see and from dangers that are hidden. According to Isaiah 59:19, Lord, I ask You to lift up a standard against the enemy on my behalf when he tries to attack me. Father, I thank You for Your faithfulness to me. I thank You for Your divine protection over my life and everyone I've prayed for today. I give You all the praise and glory. It is in Your Son Jesus' name that I pray this prayer, Amen.

Prayer for Finances

Father God, I come seeking You, my source, in the name of Jesus Christ. Lord, I come to You Jehovah Jireh, my provider, seeking Your wisdom about my finances. Father, I desire to live the life of abundance that You promised Your children in the Your word. I ask that You give me wisdom in how to be a good steward over the finances that You put in my hands. I also ask You, Lord, for witty ideas and inventions that will help me to increase what You put in my hands. Lord, I have a desire to continue to help build up Your kingdom and to be a blessing to people who are in need. I ask that You bless my finances, so that I can give and lack nothing at the same time. Father, I ask that You open the windows of Heaven and pour out blessings on my life. Fill my financial life to the overflow, I pray in Jesus' name. Lord, I ask that You remove any selfishness that I may have and anything that would stand between me using the resources You give me to help the kingdom and whoever You want me to bless. I thank You for favor. I thank You for giving me Your heart, mind, and spirit. I pray this prayer in Jesus' name. Amen.

Prayer for Health

It is with faith and thanksgiving that I come to You in the mighty name of Your Son Jesus Christ. Father God, I know that Your Son Jesus gave His life on the cross, dying for me to be free from sickness and disease. I plead the blood of Jesus over every fiber of my being. I ask that You cause the inner workings of my body to function properly in Jesus' name. Your word says in Isaiah 53:5 that Jesus was wounded for our transgressions, bruised for our iniquities, and that the chastisement of our peace was upon Him; and with His stripes we were healed. Thank You for forgiving our sin and healing all of our diseases. Father, I believe and receive what Jesus did on the cross as a finished work on my behalf. Therefore, I believe that I am healed and set free from sickness and disease. I thank that I am healed. It is in the name of Jesus that I pray this prayer and give thanks. Amen.

Prayer for Peace

I come to You, Almighty God, in Your Son Jesus' name. Lord, I come seeking refuge for my soul. My mind is tired and I'm growing weary, so I'm turning to You, the God of Peace for peace that surpasses all human understanding. You told us to cast our cares on You because You care for us, so I'm casting every care that I have on You. You are wisdom and You know what to do with my circumstances in every situation of concern. I cease from laboring to figure it out on my own. I surrender my heavy load to You and take Your yoke of peace upon me. Lord, I believe this word. I believe that You are handling everything of concern to me. Not only are You handling these concerns, but they're being perfected in Your hands. Lord, I thank You that I will now go about my day in peace. I thank You that I will have sweet sleep, in Jesus' name I pray this prayer and give thanks for the manifestation. Amen.

Prayer for Work

Lord, I come into Your presence in Your Son Jesus' name. I thank You Father for every opportunity that You've blessed me with. I thank You Lord for every open and closed door that You have for me. I thank You Lord for my job. You gave me this job for Your will and purpose, please help me to shine the light inside of me. I cast my work concerns on you. Help me to do my work diligently and to the best of my ability. I ask You for Your divine guidance on what to do in every situation. Please take all self-righteousness away from me. Help me to operate in love. Help me to be a light during this season of my life. Make it clear why I'm here; what I'm there to learn and what I'm there to teach. Bridle my tongue, keep me from idle gossip, anger, and help me to always deal fairly with my co-workers and leadership. I ask You to help us to all operate as a team. Give us all the spirit of grace to help each other at all points to do the right thing. Lord, I know every situation is in Your hands, and I thank You for it. It is in Jesus' name that I pray this prayer, Amen.

Prayer for Unsaved Family & Friends

Lord, I come to You in Your Son Jesus' name thanking You for the amazing way You love each and every one of us. Lord, I do realize that not everyone in my circle or sphere of influence knows You. So, for those that I can reach, Lord show me how to introduce them to You. I know that everyone is different, so I have to know through Your divine wisdom how to approach my unsaved friends and loved ones, and even strangers. For those that I may never have a chance to reach, Lord, I ask that You send workers in the vineyards of their lives to reach them. I ask that You send people with a heart grace to introduce them to the love of Christ that saved them from death. Father, I know that it is Your will that none will be lost; so, I thank You that Your will be done in the lives of my family and friends, and strangers who have yet to know You. I pray this prayer in Jesus' name, Amen.

These are just a few scriptures, affirmations, and prayers that I hope will help guide you in your journey. They are more in depth than you really have to go, but they may be beneficial in helping you get more specific in your prayer life. That said, I still believe one of the simplest and greatest prayers we could ever pray as believers is simply, "Help me". As our creator, God knows each of us down to the strands of hair on our heads. So, we only need to cry out to Him to get His attention. He's just like a father standing in the driveway in front of his house. When he hears his child crying after falling off his bicycle and runs to their side to help them. He wants us to call on Him. He is always here to help us.

About the Author

This self-proclaimed "country girl" has been singing since she was "knee high to a butterfly". Her vocal stylings draw from the great vocal sheroes she became accustomed to hearing growing up; from The Clark Sisters & CeeCee Winans up to today's song birds like Yolanda Adams, Kari Jobe, and Nicole C. Mullen.

Though Shay remains true to her own sound; her vocal style has been compared to the sound of Gospel great Yolanda Adams. Shay's music is filled with an ever-present message of love and hope that the world can't get too much of right now.

For her upcoming project she's working with Stellar award-winning producer, Marque Walker, who's produced for Beyoncé, Vickie Winans, & Earnest Pugh to name a few. Walker also produced Shay's debut title track "Dear Jesus". She's also slated to work with Grammy award nominated, stellar award-winning producer Stan Jones. Jones is one of the hit makers behind The Williams Brothers, Marvin Sapp, Yolanda Adams and many more.

Shay Harris is a University of Mississippi graduate. While at the university Shay sang & traveled with the University Concert Singers, Spirit Show Choir, and periodically with the Madrigal singers. She received extensive vocal training as a student on vocal scholarship.

Shay has spent more than a decade working as a highly respected & credible News Anchor, Reporter, and Photographer at major broadcast companies like ABC and Fox television. She's built a strong foundation as a television personality in Orlando, Memphis, Chattanooga, Ohio, and Texas.

During those years Shay was on the front line in urban cities covering stories of pain and heartbreak in places like Memphis, Orlando, New Orleans, and most recently Cleveland, OH where violence has left scars in communities that still haven't healed. She's also the Producer of a documentary project based on the contamination of a small rural Black community in Grenada, MS with toxic chemicals; which has garnered national attention. The case blows the whistle on yet another case that the Environmental Protection Agency has known about for years yet did nothing.

Shay has guest-starred on the syndicated hit FOX TV show "Sleepy Hollow". She will also be a Journalist/Expert on the upcoming seasons of TV One television series "Justice by Any Means" and "Fatal Attraction". From time to time you may catch appearances of Shay guest starring on reruns of the nationally syndicated shows "The Parkers" and an episode of the sitcom "The Steve Harvey Show."

Shay is currently working on her first book project "I'm Saved. Now What?" which promises to be a guide for churches in helping new converts, seasoned Christians, teens, or whomever find success in their Christian journey. If allowed it will shatter the walls of guilt, shame, and condemnation for the reader bringing them into a place of real freedom within. Some of Shay's personal life experiences are highlighted in the book. Her bouts with infirmity, bad choices, disappointment, make her identifiable and even more personable to readers.

She is available to speak and sing at churches, conferences, sporting events, and etc.

EMAIL: ShayHarrisTV@gmail.com
FACEBOOK: @shay.harris.1253
INSTAGRAM: @theshayharris
TWITTER: @IAmShayHarris
WEBSITE: www.theshayharris.com

www.ingramcontent.com/pod-product-compliance
Lightning Source LLC
Chambersburg PA
CBHW021152090426
42740CB00008B/1059